So Great Is His Love

The Best Understanding of God You Will Ever Need

Dr. Carl Branker

Foreword by Dr. Myles Munroe

Copyright © 2007 by Dr. Carl Branker

So Great Is His Love
The Best Understanding of God You Will Ever Need
by Dr. Carl Branker

Printed in the United States of America

ISBN 978-1-60266-142-4

All rights reserved solely by the author. The author guarantees all contents are original and do not infringe upon the legal rights of any other person or work. No part of this book may be reproduced in any form without the permission of the author. The views expressed in this book are not necessarily those of the publisher.

Unless otherwise indicated, Bible quotations are taken from the New King James Version. Copyright © 1979, 1980, 1982 by Thomas Nelson, Inc.

www.xulonpress.com

Contents

Dedication vii
Acknowledgments.. ix
Foreword xi
Preface... xiii
Introduction...xv

Chapter 1: An All-Inclusive Love 17
Chapter 2: The Fruit of His Spirit 31
Chapter 3: His Manner of Love 51
Chapter 4: Can God Fail Us? 57
Chapter 5: Can We Fail God? 65
Chapter 6: His Love Is Working in Us..................77
Chapter 7: How to Maintain Hope.......................85
Conclusion 95

Dedication

This book is dedicated to my darling wife, Victoria, who has always believed in my visions and words. You are my inspiration in all that I do. Thank you for working the vision with me and believing in me no matter what the situation may have looked like. Your prayers have always been a pillar of strength to me.

In memory of my grandmother, Maselline Marcano, who has gone to be with Jesus, for her words of wisdom that have kept me over the years. There are so many things she said then that I did not understand until later in life, and they have truly helped sustain me in good and bad times.

To my beloved mother, Enitha Juanita Branker, for continuing the same with an endearing love and support.

Acknowledgments

There are two men of great significance in my life whom I must acknowledge as my mentors. They are the late Bishop Turnel Nelson of Trinidad and Tobago, and my dear friend, Dr. Myles Munroe of Nassau, Bahamas. Thank you for the significance you have brought to my life over the years.

It was through our divine meeting that I was invited to be a part of the board of trustees of the International Third World Leaders Association (ITWLA), founded by Dr. Munroe. Today we still meet twice a year in the Bahamas, and our common bond of brotherly love is an enhancement to my personal and professional life.

Through the years I came to know more about my mission and purpose on this earth and decided that I would pursue it with all my heart. It was my close relationship with these two spiritual giants, Bishop Nelson and Dr. Myles, that helped refine the gifting and abilities that I didn't know existed within me at the depth of where I am today. I truly value each mentoring moment that both have deposited in my life.

Dr. Myles Munroe, thank you for birthing ITWLA. It has been the catalyst for many third world leaders to launch out and bear the mark of twenty-first century leadership. For this, I acknowledge the leadership and friendship of all my co-laborers on the ITWLA trustee board.

I also wish to acknowledge ITWLA acting executive director, Dr. Lucile Richardson, for your help in getting this project to the finish line. Thank you for being a friend.

Foreword

The most challenging experience of the human heart is the mystery of what we call unanswered prayer. Believers through the years of Christian history have stood in the face of unbelievable odds, yet steadfast, firm in faith, believing in the promises of God. There were times when I felt the Creator of the universe had forgotten me and the challenges of my little world. I often wondered whether He loved me enough to make His promises a reality.

Dr. Carl Branker, in this work, *So Great Is His Love*, captures the essence of God's love through many facets of his own trials and tribulations and journey with God. As you read this book, you will be inspired by his faith in God's love in moments of trauma.

In his simple yet profound way, Dr. Carl Branker brings the reality of human experience to this challenging subject of not just love but of God's unending love. His sound scriptural foundation serves as a guide through this perplexing topic of love through the understanding of the Creator.

It is my hope that as you read his powerful and comforting words of wisdom, you will be inspired to believe in the dark hours of life what God told you in the light. Read on and discover the truth that no matter how difficult life may become, God never fails because so great is His love.

Dr. Myles Munroe
President/Founder of Myles Munroe International
Bahamas Faith Ministries International
The International Third World Leaders Association
The International Leadership Training Institute in Nassau, Bahamas

Preface

In this era of international calamity, doom and gloom of wars, and economic and social disaster, it appears that many people are confused about the course of their life journey. Most are searching for love in all the wrong places because they have no solid foundation to rely upon when it seems as if the earth is shaking beneath their feet.

Today there is no lack of churches and ministries for people to find and settle in to be taught the Word of God so they can grow up spiritually. Yet, it is sad to observe how believers are being attacked in every area of life so much until they find it difficult to get up again after feeling they failed God or God failed them. The tragedies of life have left them without an understanding of God's love for them in good times and particularly in bad times.

Several years ago while praying, I had a vision of God weeping, and I said, "Lord, why are You weeping?" He said, "My son, the world is yet to hear the message of My love." I pondered that statement for a moment before asking God how it could be. He said, "There are a lot of messages being taught around the world, yet the world is not grasping My true love. If people could receive the knowledge of My unconditional love and experience it through My children, they would flock to the church."

I never forgot that vision, and so I stepped forward in teaching several series about God's love, hoping that those hearing the message would be transformed. In so doing, others would not only see but also experience God's love in their lives.

I am writing this book because I believe people are searching for love more than anything else, yet it is something that has been given to us since the foundations of the world. I want them to know that in order to find love, they must come to know God, for He is love. It is in those moments of searching that we need the assurance that we can run to God and feel His unending love.

So Great Is His Love attempts to define God's nature and character. If we learn these great attributes, we will discover our true selves and our divine destiny in the world.

Introduction

The writer George D. Watson in his book, *Our Own God*, wrote, "It is a beautiful task to study God. The human mind can never be employed on any subject as full of rich reward as when trying to find out the knowledge of God. To search after the character and perfection of God is the highest science, the deepest philosophy, the loftiest poetry, the sublimest history, the truest theology and the most thrilling biography."

No human love can set the standard for understanding God's agape love, but the Spirit of God is responsible for imparting the will to love upon us. To grasp the true knowledge of God leads us into the highest understanding of the greatness of His love. Even as we read the accounts of Christ in the gospels, it becomes easier to understand God's love. To aid us further in understanding His agape love, we must fully understand God's nature, that is His "essence" or "substance," and it includes all that

He is, that uniquely makes Him God. Thus we will examine how God demonstrates His love for us.

The apostle Paul gives the best illustration of God's love in Romans 5:8: "But God demonstrates His own love toward us, in that while we were still sinners, Christ died for us." It says something spectacular happened not when we received Christ in our heart, but while we were still sinners Christ did something for us that no other god has ever done. He laid down His life because so great was His love for the whole world.

This journey into *So Great Is His Love* explores that beautiful task of studying God to bring a deeper revelation of why He never fails.

Chapter 1

An All-Inclusive Love

During my children's early years, I recall an incident in our neighborhood that involved one of our neighbors being assisted by an ambulance, a fire truck, and the police. My son, Jonathan, and I were taking a walk when we saw the commotion, and Jonathan asked, "Papa, what happened?" I said "Well, Jonathan, I don't know," and he kept on asking the same question over and over again. So I told him that apparently someone had gotten hurt. He said, "Someone got hurt—well, I hope their daddy is home."

I was touched by that statement, because in the mind of a three-year-old it meant that if daddy is home then everything would be all right. And I said to God, "Daddy, thank You that You are always home."

In this world of senseless tragedies, calamities, wars, confusion, and social unrest, it is good to know that we have someone who loves us and cares about each and every little thing in our lives. We see His love in the birth, life, and death of Jesus. The New Testament scripture tells us in John 3:16, "For God so loved the world that He gave His only begotten Son, that whoever believes in Him should not perish but have everlasting life."

Agape Love

The Greek word for love here is *agape*. The word is written in the form of a superlative, to make it known that this love of God is the most supreme, highest, and greatest act of love. It is an all-inclusive love to save, heal, deliver, set free, and protect.

We don't have the capacity to love anyone apart from the love of God. Spouses cannot love each other apart from the love of God. Parents cannot love their children rightly apart from the love of God. Children cannot love their parents apart from the love of God. Siblings cannot love each other apart rightly from the love of God.

That four-letter word is small but most powerful. It says that the perfect love of God is extended to a world of imperfection, degeneration, condemnation, and disgrace. I don't know about you, but I am so glad that God so loves me!

Love must show action just as love must act, because it is an action word. Love proves itself by what it does. God so loved the world that He gave.

That is action! He did not give because the world was worthy. He did not give because the world was needy. He gave because He so loved! That is grace! In this act of love is an example of divine giving.

The Old Testament book of Hosea gives rare insight into the heart of God. In this book, God tells the people that He loves them and that He has loved them as a faithful husband and a perfect Father.

Hosea 11:1 says, "When Israel was a child, I loved him, and out of Egypt I called My son."

Verses 3-4 tell us, "I taught Ephraim to walk, taking them by their arms; but they did not know that I healed them. I drew them with gentle cords, with bands of love, and I was to them as those who take the yoke from their neck. I stooped and fed them." Hosea 13:4-5 states, "Yet I am the LORD your God ever since the land of Egypt, and you shall know no God but Me; for there is no savior besides Me. I knew you in the wilderness, in the land of great drought."

God describes His relationship with us by revealing His love for us. He opens up His heart and reveals the depth of love He has for us. These words to Israel are also words to you and me. He has patiently cared for us, taught us to walk, and fed us. He has led us out of the Egypt of our sin into the promised land of our salvation. He repeatedly sets us back on the right course while being very gracious and merciful. One ought to wonder how He can love as much as He does.

But how did Israel respond to the love of God? How did they react to being chosen by God as His beloved? Hosea 2:4-5 tells us that she was unfaithful.

She chased after other lovers. Israel worshipped Baal, the god of the Canaanites. And she believed that Baal would provide food and water and all her needs.

As parents who faithfully provide for our children, it hurts us when they run to others to get that which we have faithfully provided and still want to give them. Likewise, it's sad to know that when God's name is mentioned in the world or in the church, the first thing that comes to mind for most people is "dread"—dread in the sense that when people measure their lives against who God is, most times in that split second their thoughts bring them into condemnation regarding their disposition in life. Some hands may go up in the air with voices shouting, "Oh, how I love the Lord." Others may be less enthusiastic because they are thinking about their last sin.

It is not unusual to feel a sense of conviction when the name of the Lord is mentioned. Some think everything about God except that He loves them. When we hear the name of the Lord, we should be more excited than when we hear the name of our lover. It should have a profound effect on our soul, mind, spirit, and body, especially as children of God.

He Loves

The main message of God is that He loves. This basic message was not conveyed to the world by the lifestyle of the people who were supposed to carry the banner and the message of God's love. Let us look at Exodus 17:1-4: "Then all the congregation of the children of Israel set out on their journey from the Wilderness of Sin, according to the commandment of the LORD, and camped in Rephidim; but there was no water for the people to drink. Therefore the people contended with Moses, and said, "Give us water that we may drink." So Moses said to them, "Why do you contend with me? Why do you tempt the LORD?" And the people thirsted there for water, and the people complained against Moses, and said, "Why is it you have brought us up out of Egypt, to kill us and our children and our livestock with thirst?" So Moses cried out to the LORD, saying, "What shall I do with this people? They are almost ready to stone me!"

Remember, they are in the hot, howling desert, and God has preserved them, fed them, and taken care of them all the way, and suddenly they became thirsty. Out of our needs or out of our lack comes the greatest opportunity to trust God. However, instead of believing and trusting God, we complain and create more confusion. When we complain, we create a force against ourselves. Words have power.

The children of Israel failed to remember how God had blessed them and brought them out of Egypt. All they knew was that they were thirsty and had no water. So they attacked their leader, the person God used to bring them out, the one who brought them across the sea and stood in the face of pharaoh for them.

When they found that there was no water, they quickly picked up stones in their hands, ready to stone Moses to death. Exodus 17:5-6 says, "And the LORD said to Moses, 'Go on before the people, and take with you some of the elders of Israel. Also take in your hand your rod with which you struck the river, and go. Behold, I will stand before you there on the rock in Horeb; and you shall strike the rock, and water will come out of it, that the people may drink.' And Moses did so in the sight of the elders of Israel."

Now that was not a good thing for Moses to do, because he was responding to the people's murmuring. As a result, God instructed him to go back. Now remember God was on the Mount of Horeb and where God is, everything around that place becomes holy. For instance, if you put a dead man upon the rock where God was, he would come to life. If you put a rock there, the rock would be able to cry out and declare that God is holy. So Moses had to take the rod and hit the rock, which was holy as a result of God's presence. We know it was holy because this is the same mount where God spoke to Moses. Therefore, when Moses struck the rock, he was actually striking God in the presence of everyone.

God could have told Moses to just speak to the rock as He did before, and the rock would have brought forth water. But the Lord said He would take full responsibility and in the midst of their wicked mindset and murderous spirit, they obtained love in the form of their thirst being quenched.

Verse 7 continues: "So he called the name of the place Massah and Meribah, because of the contention of the children of Israel, and because they tempted the LORD, saying, 'Is the LORD among us or not?'" Can you imagine your child coming to you and saying,

"Look, mom, dad, are you going to feed me or not?" Then you respond by saying, "Here, eat!" Not only was the Lord with them, but He fed them even in the midst of contention. It is His great love that overrides our faults and failures.

A Taste of God's Love

The Israelites tested God's love with their constant murmurings while they were in the wilderness. They tested God's servant, Moses, until Moses ignored God's command and struck the rock at Marah to get water for them. The water that the rock produced was bitter. That was meant to serve as a reminder of the bitter life and the struggles they experienced while in bondage in Egypt.

God provided food and water for the Israelites on a daily basis over the forty years that they wandered in the desert. Despite God's daily provision of quails and manna, the Israelites protested, cried, and lusted after the fish, the cucumbers and melons, the leeks and the onions that they ate while they were in Egypt.

When God provided the manna to the children of Israel, He was pouring out bits of Himself in the form of the white frost, but the Israelites were too self-absorbed to recognize His love, steadfastness, and goodness to them. Exodus 16:14 describes manna this way: "And when the dew that lay was gone up, behold, upon the face of the wilderness there lay a small round thing, as small as the hoar frost on the ground" (KJV).

Their eyes were not open to the outpouring of God's spirit through the manna, and their hearts were not open to a relationship with Him, but God began to introduce Himself in a different way. He knew the Israelites had heard of Him through the prophets and that He spoke to them through Moses and Aaron, so He wanted them to experience Him and His true love in an unforgettable manner. Through the manna, God gave the Israelites the experience of a taste that they had never before had in a meal. It was a taste that could only be equated with God's love.

Exodus 16:31-32 says, "And the house of Israel called the name therefore Manna: and it was like coriander seed, white; and the taste of it was like wafers made with honey. And Moses said, 'This is the thing that the Lord commandeth, Fill an omer of it to be kept for your generations; that they may see the bread wherewith I have fed you in the wilderness, when I brought you forth from the land of Egypt.'"

Verse 35 tells us, "And the children of Israel did eat manna forty years, until they came to a land inhabited, they did eat manna, until they came unto the borders of the land of Caanan" (KJV).

The last meal that the Israelites ate in Egypt was one of bitter herbs, which signified the last taste of struggle and the gall of oppression. When God provided the first meal of manna in the wilderness, it was in stark contrast to their last meal in Egypt. It was sweet like honey. God wanted the Israelites to associate His provision for them with the sweet taste of honey. It was the first time they experienced a taste in direct contrast to anything they had tasted in Egypt. It represented God's love.

It took a generation of forty years to come to know of God's love, to taste of the sweetness of His unconditional love and to trust His love to bring them through various situations that they encountered. Many of us are like the Israelites; we have tasted of God's love and fellowship, but we are distracted by religion and tradition. These have catapulted us back into bad habits and negative influences that produce worms in our lives, just like the manna rotted and produced worms when the Israelites exhibited greed and disobeyed God's instruction.

In Psalm 19, the psalmist David extols the purity of God's love, His righteousness, the perfection of His law, and the wisdom of God. In verse 10, he declares, "More to be desired are they than gold, yea, than much fine gold: sweeter also than honey and the honeycomb" (KJV). We are encouraged to return to our first love, since His love, His precepts, and His wisdom are more profitable to our lives than material possessions.

At the present time, our world is plagued by wars, strange illnesses, and social and moral turbulence. The Eastern world is mired in the devastation of war; the Western world is fragmented in its allegiance to the warring sides in the East; and the developing world is inundated with crime and corruption. Families are torn apart, and society is under siege. It is a time when many wonder about God's love in the midst of this chaos.

Our personal lives are challenged on a daily basis, and our walk with God, as Christians, is equally tested. Despite what we see, we should not allow time, religious differences, or adverse circumstances to mar the remembrance of the taste of God's love. It is His true love that has no equal, a love that no one else can give. God so loved the world that He gave His only begotten Son to redeem us. Jesus is our hope for today and the future.

In John 6:31-33, Jesus reminds us of the Father's love for us, the same love that the Israelites experienced in the wilderness. John wrote, "Our fathers did eat manna in the desert; as it is written, He gave them bread from heaven to eat. Then Jesus said unto them, Verily, verily, I say unto you, Moses gave you not that bread from heaven; but my Father giveth you true bread from heaven. For the bread of God is he which cometh down from heaven and giveth life unto the world" (KJV).

In the Song of Solomon 2:4, the Shulamite told the daughters of Jerusalem, "He brought me to the banqueting house, and his banner over me was love." The word "banner" is Jehova-Nissi, meaning "God's banner over us."

During the ancient days when kings went out to war, they would carry an insignia, a flag or staff that bore the mark of the king. In the heat of a battle the soldiers would look to see if their flag was flying, and if it was, it served as source of encouragement to keep on fighting. The philosophy back then was that if the king's symbol was not flying high during battle, it was a sign that they were losing the battle.

Have you ever seen movies in which men still fought with swords, spears, armor, and shields? They always carried a flag in the midst of battle. If the enemy knocked their flag over, someone would run to put it back to its rightful position.

God wanted Israel to know that He was going to wipe out the Amalekites just to prove His own banner was flying high over them in every battle. Despite what they did to God, He kept His promise to them.

From One Heart to Another

First John 4:7-11 says, "Beloved, let us love one another, for love is of God; and everyone who loves is born of God and knows God. He who does not love does not know God, for God is love. In this the love of God was manifested toward us, that God has sent His only begotten Son into the world, that we might live through Him. In this is love, not that we loved God, but that He loved us and sent His Son to be the propitiation for our sins. Beloved, if God so loved us, we also ought to love one another."

Love is not measured by the amount of times you say "I love you" or the amount of times you give flowers. Love is something that flows from one person's heart to another. To know God is to know His love.

The world has blinded us to the true meaning of a pure heart that loves. First we must understand that God's love is pure, not filled with jealousy, pride, but loves what is good and right. Above all, God's love covers a multitude of sins.

Everyone has a heart that can love. Everyone has love; you can love, and you can give love. The inability to love is a choice. There is so much more joy in giving love than in receiving it. There are more blessings in loving someone than in being loved. Every person born of God has love in his or her heart. Only the devil and his demons cannot love.

You may have committed adultery or fornicated last night, but God's loving heart towards you was still to wake you up and allow you to come to work with His protective banner over you.

God has a heart that loves us despite our wronging each other and despite having the long trailer of problems in our lives. There is nothing more valuable in this world than agape, God's love—not your money, house, boat, car, job, and other earthly possessions. It is up to us to make a decision to love from the bottom of our heart.

You must forgive as the Father forgives us daily. Forgive all who have wronged you. Release the bitterness in your heart and make a decision to love those who hate you and those you hate. It is time for us to show the world that we are rich with the most valuable asset—love.

First John 4:17-18 says, "In this way, love is made complete among us so that we will have confidence on the Day of Judgment because in this world we are like him. There is no fear in love. But perfect love drives out fear, because fear has to do with punishment. The one who fears is not made perfect in love" (NIV). If we are afraid of judgment, it means our heart has not been made perfect. Right now we need to search the condition of our heart.

It is a shame that some children don't know their parents' love. My father never hugged me, but his parents never hugged him. But you don't have to continue with the same thing from past generations. You can make a change now to take on a heart that loves as God so loved the whole world.

Chapter 2

The Fruit of His Spirit

The Bible tells us in 1 John 4:8 that "God is Love." So out of that love will manifest the other eight characteristics of the Spirit of God. John 15:12-14 says, "This is My commandment, that you love one another as I have loved you. Greater love has no one than this, than to lay down one's life for his friends. You are My friends if you do whatever I command you." Jesus gave this commandment regarding us loving our neighbors as ourselves. The greatest force, power, act, or demonstration of this love is when people can see God's love flowing through others.

The Bible confirms this in John 15:5: "I am the vine; you are the branches. If a man remains in me and I in him, he will bear much fruit; apart from me you can do nothing." Each of the nine fruit or character traits can be seen in the life of Christ. He is our model for leading a fruitful life. John 15:4 says, "Remain in me, and I will remain in you. No branch can bear fruit by itself; it must remain in the vine. Neither can you bear fruit unless you remain in me."

In Galatians 5:22, the apostle Paul speaks about the fruit of the Spirit. He says, "But the fruit of the Spirit is love, joy, peace, longsuffering, kindness, goodness, faithfulness, gentleness, self-control. Against such there is no law." He was writing to the Christians in Galatia, who were trying to decide whether non-Jewish converts should be circumcised. Paul said it is not necessary (Gal. 5:6). In Galatians 5:1, he reminded them that they had been set free from the law. To prevent any further confusion, Paul attempts to enlighten the Christians about the characteristics of God's Spirit through the illustration of His character traits.

There are sixty-seven verses in the New Testament that relate to fruit; fifty-four come from the same root Greek word *harpazdo*, which translates as "to catch, to seize, to take by force." The word "fruit" is singular, and yet nine things are listed. That is because the Greek shows the singular. When using the singular, it shows that all believers are to have all of these items, unlike the gifts of the Spirit.

Fruit is not something we do, and we cannot bear fruit on our own, for it comes only from the Holy Spirit. The true marks of our spirituality and the signs of maturity in Christian growth are found not in the gifts of the Spirit but in producing the fruit of the Spirit. The apostle Paul in 1 Corinthians 13 told the people at Corinth that if we do not have love, which is a fruit of the Spirit, then we are just making noise like a clanging cymbal. He says we have nothing if we do not have love. So we need to examine the greatness of God's love by looking at His fruit.

Let us examine each of the nine fruit, beginning with love.

Love

There are four Greek words for our one word "love." They are:
1. *Eros*: physical love (motivated by pleasure)
2. *Stergo*: love between people and a ruler (motivated by authority/title/position)
3. *Phileo*: brotherly love (motivated by affection/fondness)
4. *Agape*: unconditional love (motivated by Christ)

The Bible tells us that God is the originator of love ("God is Love," 1 John 4:6). First John 4:7, 9-10 says, "For love is from God...By this the love of God was manifested in us that God has sent His only begotten Son into the world so that we might live through Him. In this is love, not that we loved God, but that He loved us and sent His Son to be a propitiation for our sins." John 3:16 says, "For God so loved the world that He gave His only begotten Son, that whoever believes in Him should not perish, but have everlasting life." Romans 5:8 says, "But God demonstrates His own love for us, in that while we were yet sinners, Christ died for us." And finally, John 17:26 says, "So that the love with which you have loved Me may be in them, and I in them."

This type of love characterizes God. It is His infinite attribute. That is, He assists us in receiving this love through Jesus Christ and His death on the Cross, which was only attained through Him. This is also the type of love that God requires us to give back to Him as well as give to the world.

Love for God

Deuteronomy 6:5-6: "You shall love the LORD your God with all your heart, with all your soul, and with all your strength. And these words which I command you today shall be in your heart."

Deuteronomy 10:12: "And now, Israel, what does the LORD your God require of you, but to fear the LORD your God, to walk in all His ways and to love Him, to serve the LORD your God with all your heart and with all your soul."

1 John 5:3: "For this is the love of God, that we keep His commandments. And His commandments are not burdensome." Knowing this love is "natural" for God means it must be acquired by us. That also means acknowledging what God did for us in Jesus.

Matthew 22:39: "You shall love your neighbor as yourself."

Love for Man

John 13:34-35: "A new commandment I give to you, that you love one another; as I have loved you, that you also love one another. By this all will know that you are My disciples, if you have love for one another."

John 15:12: "This is My commandment, that you love one another as I have loved you."

Romans 13:8: "Owe no one anything except to love one another, for he who loves another has fulfilled the law. "

Ephesians 5:2: "And walk in love, as Christ also has loved us and given Himself for us, an offering and a sacrifice to God for a sweet-smelling aroma."

1 John 3:11: "For this is the message that you heard from the beginning, that we should love one another, "For this is the message which you have heard from the beginning, that we should love one another."

1 John 3:14: "We know that we have passed from death to life, because we love the brethren. He who does not love his brother abides in death. 'We know that we have passed out of death into life, because we love the brethren. He who does not love abides in death.'"

1 John 3:16-17: "By this we know love, because He laid down His life for us. And we also ought to lay down our lives for the brethren. But whoever has this world's goods, and sees his brother in need, and shuts up his heart from him, how does the love of God abide in him?"

1 John 3:23: "And this is His commandment: that we should believe on the name of His Son Jesus Christ and love one another, as He gave us commandment."

1 John 4:7: "Beloved, let us love one another, for love is of God; and everyone who loves is born of God and knows God."

1 John 4:11: "Beloved, if God so loved us, we also ought to love one another."

1 John 4:20-21: "If someone says, 'I love God,' and hates his brother, he is a liar; for he who does not love his brother whom he has seen, how can he love God whom he has not seen? And this commandment we have from Him: that he who loves God must love his brother also."

God commands the agape love from us, and He also requires *phileo* love. We are quick to love with our head before our heart, which leads into an emotional love that depends on how we feel. Loving from the heart shows an attitude that desires the well-being of everyone. This is shown best in the example of Jesus' discourse with Peter after His resurrection, before His ascension. John 21:15-17 says, "So when they had eaten breakfast, Jesus said to Simon Peter, 'Simon, son of Jonah, do you love Me more than these?' He said to Him, 'Yes, Lord; You know that I love You.' He said to him, 'Feed My lambs.' He said to him again a second time, 'Simon, son of Jonah, do you love Me?' He said to Him, 'Yes, Lord; You know that I love You.' He said to him, 'Tend My sheep.' He said to him the third time, 'Simon, son of Jonah, do you love Me?' Peter was grieved because He said to him the third time, 'Do you love Me?' And he said to Him, 'Lord, You know all things; You know that I love You.' Jesus said to him, Feed My sheep.'"

Love is best defined by the apostle Paul in 1 Corinthians 13:4-8 and 13: "Love is patient, love is kind and is not jealous; love does not brag and is not arrogant, does not act unbecomingly; it does not seek its own, is not provoked, does not take into account a wrong suffered, does not rejoice in unrighteousness, but rejoices with the truth; bears all things, believes all things, hopes all things, endures all things. Love never fails…But now faith, hope, love, abide these three; but the greatest of these is love." (NAS).

Joy

The dictionary defines joy as "exultation of spirit; gladness; delight." Joy does mean not happiness, which is an emotion that depends on positive circumstances or situations.

Joy is an eternal characteristic of God. Malachi 3:6 says, "For I am the LORD, I do not change." His eternal characteristic of joy remains constant and steadfast no matter what the circumstances or situation might possess. This is best illustrated in the life of Christ.

Hebrews 12:2: "Looking unto Jesus, the author and finisher of our faith, who for the joy that was set before Him endured the cross, despising the shame, and has sat down at the right hand of the throne of God."

Psalms 16:11: "You will show me the path of life; in Your presence is fullness of joy; at Your right hand are pleasures forevermore."

James 1:2-4: "My brethren, count it all joy when you fall into various trials, knowing that the testing of your faith produces patience. But let patience have its perfect work, that you may be perfect and complete, lacking nothing."

Peace

Shalom (peace) was the usual word of greeting or farewell in both the Old Testament and New Testament. It usually means "freedom from strife, whether internal or external." It also means "security from outward enemies as well as calm of heart."

Jesus is our model of peace. Mark 4:37-39 says, "And a great windstorm arose, and the waves beat into the boat, so that it was already filling. But He was in the stern, asleep on a pillow. And they awoke Him and said to Him, 'Teacher, do You not care that we are perishing?' Then He arose and rebuked the wind, and said to the sea, 'Peace, be still!' And the wind ceased and there was a great calm."

Psalm 119:165: "Great peace have those who love Your law, and nothing causes them to stumble."

Romans 5:1: "Therefore, having been justified by faith, we have peace with God through our Lord Jesus Christ."

Romans 5:11: "And not only that, but we also rejoice in God through our Lord Jesus Christ, through whom we have now received the reconciliation."

Colossians 1:20: "And by Him to reconcile all things to Himself, by Him, whether things on earth or things in heaven, having made peace through the blood of His cross."

Through our faith in Jesus Christ and His atoning death on the cross we are reconciled to God. Because we have peace with God, His peace becomes available to us!

We have the peace of God, which is defined as "a sense of calm and complete absence of hostility and fear in the heart. This peace in our Lord is shown in Isaiah 9:6: "For unto us a Child is born, unto us a Son is given; and the government will be upon His shoulder. And His name will be called Wonderful, Counselor, Mighty God, Everlasting Father, Prince of Peace."

John 14:27: "Peace I leave with you, My peace I give to you; not as the world gives do I give to you. Let not your heart be troubled, neither let it be afraid."

Philippians 4:6: "Be anxious for nothing, but in everything by prayer and supplication, with thanksgiving, let your requests be made known to God; and the peace of God, which surpasses all understanding, will guard your hearts and minds through Christ Jesus."

I Peter 5:7: "Casting all your care upon Him, for He cares for you."

Colossians 3:15: "Let the peace of Christ rule in your hearts, to which indeed you were called in one body; and be thankful." We cannot trust God when we are worrying.

Isaiah 26:3: "You will keep him in perfect peace, whose mind is stayed on You, because he trusts in

You." This perfect peace comes from a trusting love relationship with God.

Matthew 5:9: "Blessed are the peacemakers, for they shall be called sons of God." We must also be at peace with man.

Hebrews 12:14: "Pursue peace with all people, and holiness, without which no one will see the Lord."

2 Corinthians 13:11: "Finally, brethren, farewell. Become complete. Be of good comfort, be of one mind, live in peace; and the God of love and peace will be with you."

Patience

Patience is a characteristic of God demonstrated in the Old Testament and New Testament. The New Testament "patience" carries two basic ideas or principles. The first is "bearing up under suffering or despair," and the other suggests "self-restraint in the face of unsatisfied desires."

2 Peter 3:9: "The Lord is not slack concerning His promise, as some count slackness, but is longsuffering toward us, not willing that any should perish but that all should come to repentance. But the ones that fell on the good ground are those who, having heard the word with a noble and good heart, keep it and bear fruit with patience."

Luke 8:15: "But the ones that fell on the good ground are those who, having heard the word with a noble and good heart, keep it and bear fruit with patience."

Ecclesiastes 7:8: "The end of a thing is better than its beginning; the patient in spirit is better than the proud in spirit."

Colossians 1:11: "Strengthened with all might, according to His glorious power, for all patience and longsuffering with joy."

Ephesians 4:2: "With all lowliness and gentleness, with longsuffering, bearing with one another in love."

Colossians 3:12-13: "Therefore, as the elect of God, holy and beloved, put on tender mercies, kindness, humility, meekness, longsuffering; bearing with one another, and forgiving one another, if anyone has a complaint against another; even as Christ forgave you, so you also must do." The fruit of patience means leading and living a forgiven as well as a forgiving life.

Romans 5:3-4: "And not only that, but we also glory in tribulations, knowing that tribulation produces perseverance; and perseverance, character; and character, hope."

Hebrews 10:36: "For you have need of endurance, so that after you have done the will of God, you may receive the promise."

James 1:3-4: "Knowing that the testing of your faith produces patience. But let patience have its perfect work, that you may be perfect and complete, lacking nothing."

1 Peter 2:20: "For what credit is it if, when you are beaten for your faults, you take it patiently? But when you do good and suffer, if you take it patiently, this is commendable before God."

Kindness

Here we will look at God's kindness towards man, which is revealed in His Son, Jesus Christ.

Psalm 117:2: "For His merciful kindness is great toward us."

Ephesians 2:6-7: "And raised us up together, and made us sit together in the heavenly places in Christ Jesus, that in the ages to come He might show the exceeding riches of His grace in His kindness toward us in Christ Jesus."

Titus 3:4-5: "But when the kindness and the love of God our Savior toward man appeared, not by works of righteousness which we have done, but according to His mercy He saved us."

The fruit of kindness can be found at least fifty times throughout the Bible. This fruit has several different elements. True kindness is gentle. The symbol of the Holy Spirit is the dove, a non-quarreling bird. Kindness is often shown as the opposite of quarrelsome. It is also found in the context of servanthood.

2 Timothy 2:24: "And a servant of the Lord must not quarrel but be gentle to all, able to teach, patient."

2 Corinthians 6:4-6: "But in all things we commend ourselves as ministers of God: in much patience, in tribulations, in needs, in distresses, in stripes, in imprisonments, in tumults, in labors, in sleeplessness, in fastings; by purity, by knowledge, by longsuffering, by kindness, by the Holy Spirit, by sincere love."

True kindness is compassionate and shows empathy. Sympathy is "feeling sorry for" while empathy is "feeling sorry with."

Philippians 2:5,7: Let this mind be in you which was also in Christ Jesus…but made Himself of no reputation, taking the form of a bondservant, and coming in the likeness of men."

Colossians 3:12: "Therefore, as the elect of God, holy and beloved, put on tender mercies, kindness, humility, meekness, longsuffering."

True kindness is forgiving, and it brings us to repentance. When we offer kindness rather than bitterness, this shows the character of God and leads to repentance.

Romans 2:4: "Or do you despise the riches of His goodness, forbearance, and longsuffering, not knowing that the goodness of God leads you to repentance?"

Ephesians 4:32: "And be kind to one another, tenderhearted, forgiving one another, even as God in Christ forgave you."

True kindness redirects and restores:

Galatians 6:1: "Brethren, if a man is overtaken in any trespass, you who are spiritual restore such a one in a spirit of gentleness, considering yourself lest you also be tempted."

Psalm 141:5: "Let the righteous strike me; it shall be a kindness. And let him rebuke me; it shall be as excellent oil; let my head not refuse it. For still my prayer is against the deeds of the wicked."

Acts 28:2: "And the natives showed us unusual kindness; for they kindled a fire and made us all welcome, because of the rain that was falling and because of the cold."

Goodness

The Bible refers to goodness as being more than just the avoidance of evil.

Exodus 33:18-19: "And he said, 'Please, show me Your glory.' Then He said, 'I will make all My goodness pass before you, and I will proclaim the name of the LORD before you. I will be gracious to whom I will be gracious, and I will have compassion on whom I will have compassion.'"

God's goodness reveals the idea of His sovereignty and His nature. God's goodness shines from within us.

Ephesians 5:9: "For the fruit of the Spirit is in all goodness, righteousness, and truth."

Matthew 5:16: "Let your light so shine before men, that they may see your good works and glorify your Father in heaven."

Romans 12:9: "Let love be without hypocrisy. Abhor what is evil. Cling to what is good."

Romans 12:21: "Do not be overcome by evil, but overcome evil with good."

Galatians 6:10: "Therefore, as we have opportunity, let us do good to all, especially to those who are of the household of faith."

Colossians 1:10: "That you may walk worthy of the Lord, fully pleasing Him, being fruitful in every good work and increasing in the knowledge of God;"

2 Thessalonians 1:11: "Therefore we also pray always for you that our God would count you worthy of this calling, and fulfill all the good pleasure of His goodness and the work of faith with power."

1 Peter 2:12: "Having your conduct honorable among the Gentiles, that when they speak against you as evildoers, they may, by your good works which they observe, glorify God in the day of visitation."

Faithfulness

Faithfulness must be demonstrated in our daily lives. It is a direct result of our love relationship with the Lord.

Proverbs 3:3: "Having your conduct honorable among the Gentiles, that when they speak against you as evildoers, they may, by your good works which they observe, glorify God in the day of visitation."

The word faithful, or one of its derivatives, is found 109 times in the Bible. It is used in the Old Testament to mean stability and truth, to be true or certain.

Isaiah 30:21: "Your ears shall hear a word behind you, saying, 'This is the way, walk in it,' whenever you turn to the right hand or whenever you turn to the left."

In the New Testament it is used as trustworthy, sure, and true. It is also used as a verb meaning to convince by inward certainty.

Revelation 1:5: "And from Jesus Christ, the faithful witness, the firstborn from the dead, and the ruler over the kings of the earth. To Him who loved us and washed us from our sins in His own blood."

Faithfulness requires much pain in the process of obtaining God's blessings. It emphasizes being trustworthy, loyal, and reliable, and the ability to remain steadfast.

Proverbs 28:20: "A faithful man will abound with blessings, but he who hastens to be rich will not go unpunished."

Revelation 2:10: "Do not fear any of those things which you are about to suffer. Indeed, the devil is about to throw some of you into prison, that you may be tested, and you will have tribulation ten days. Be faithful until death, and I will give you the crown of life."

Jesus rebuked the religious sect of their time for their lack of faithfulness. Matthew 23:23 says, "Woe to you, scribes and Pharisees, hypocrites! For you pay tithe of mint and anise and cumin, and have neglected the weightier matters of the law: justice and mercy and faith. These you ought to have done, without leaving the others undone."

Faithfulness must be demonstrated in every area of our Christian lives. Matthew 25 tells us about the parable of the talents.

Matthew 16:10-12: "'Nor the seven loaves of the four thousand and how many large baskets you took up? How is it you do not understand that I did not speak to you concerning bread?—but to beware of the leaven of the Pharisees and Sadducees.' Then they understood that He did not tell them to beware of the leaven of bread, but of the doctrine of the Pharisees and Sadducees."

Gentleness

In the Septuagint (an ancient translation of the Hebrew Old Testament into Greek), the word "gentleness" is translated and used as "one who is humble in disposition and character; one who is submissive under the divine will." The English translation of "gentleness" refers to "meekness," suggesting the submission to another without the resistance to the wrongs of others.

There are two New Testament definitions of "gentleness." One is used in the context of man's gentleness, and the other is used in the context of God's gentleness. Man's gentleness refers to kindness and meekness. God's gentleness refers to the appropriate timing for the mild patience of God to be shown.

2 Samuel 22:36: "You have also given me the shield of Your salvation; Your gentleness has made me great."

David recalls the gentleness of God, as in Psalm 18:35: "You have also given me the shield of Your salvation; Your right hand has held me up, Your gentleness has made me great."

The word meekness is also used to show gentleness, and it does not mean "weakness." Rather, it carries with it the meaning of "strength under control."

Matthew 5:5: "Blessed are the meek, for they shall inherit the earth."

Matthew 11:29: "Take My yoke upon you and learn from Me, for I am gentle and lowly in heart, and you will find rest for your souls."

Ephesians 4:2: "With all lowliness and gentleness, with longsuffering, bearing with one another in love."

Colossians 3:12: "Therefore, as the elect of God, holy and beloved, put on tender mercies, kindness, humility, meekness, longsuffering."

Self-Control

The last fruit of the Spirit, or characteristic of God, listed in Galatians 5:22-23 is that of self-control. The King James Version refers to this as temperance. It means to have "mastery over one's own desires and impulses." The New Testament translation of self-control means "to have an inward strength."

1 Peter 2:11: "Beloved, I beg you as sojourners and pilgrims, abstain from fleshly lusts which war against the soul."

Our physical longings and cravings must also be kept under control. The apostle Paul challenges us concerning this:

1 Corinthians 6:12: "All things are lawful for me, but all things are not helpful."

Hebrews 12:1: "Therefore we also, since we are surrounded by so great a cloud of witnesses, let us lay aside every weight, and the sin which so easily ensnares us, and let us run with endurance the race that is set before us."

Self-control must be displayed in our anger and how we speak.

James 1:26: "If anyone among you thinks he is religious, and does not bridle his tongue but deceives his own heart, this one's religion is useless."

James 3:2: "For we all stumble in many things. If anyone does not stumble in word, he is a perfect man, able also to bridle the whole body."

Self-control must be used when making decisions, for it will reveal the mood swings that are often revealed in us. Peter admonishes us to use self-control, giving all diligence.

2 Peter 1:5-11: "But also for this very reason, giving all diligence, add to your faith virtue, to virtue knowledge, to knowledge self-control, to self-control perseverance, to perseverance godliness, to godliness brotherly kindness, and to brotherly kindness love. For if these things are yours and abound, you will be neither barren nor unfruitful in the knowledge of our Lord Jesus Christ. For he who lacks these things is shortsighted, even to blindness, and has forgotten that he was cleansed from his old sins. Therefore, brethren, be even more diligent to make your call and election sure, for if you do these things you will never stumble; for so an entrance will be supplied to you abundantly into the everlasting kingdom of our Lord and Savior Jesus Christ."

May these nine character traits of God become more eminent in our lives as we strive to live according to His ways that have been set before us.

As we take on more of His character, then our sinful nature will have to decrease. Thus, the world will see us as examples of Christ and have reason to want to follow us as we share the greatness of His love for the whole world.

Chapter 3

His Manner of Love

First John 3:1 says, "Behold what manner of love the Father has bestowed on us, that we should be called children of God! Therefore the world does not know us, because it did not know Him. Beloved, now we are children of God; and it has not yet been revealed what we shall be, but we know that when He is revealed, we shall be like Him, for we shall see Him as He is. And everyone who has this hope in Him purifies himself, just as He is pure."

John says "behold" as meaning to take note, become aware at the manner in which God's love is being shown to us. The word "manner" refers to something beyond the ordinary or that which we are not used to experiencing in our lives.

Matthew 8:27 and Mark 4:41 tell how the disciples were amazed when they saw how Jesus calmed the storm and raging sea. They said, "What manner of man is this, that even the winds and the sea obey him!" They saw an ability and power exhibited by Jesus that they had never seen before and could not imagine ever seeing it demonstrated at that level.

They disciples experienced God's love beyond the ordinary. It was not of this world just as God's love is out of this world. It always makes us shout "Wow!"

What Manner of Names

God's manner of love is known by the names that express Him. We can see from the list below that His love goes beyond all boundaries in order for Him to be Lord, which means "owner." If He owns us, then He must take care of us. We must be sufficient in Him, meaning we do not need anything or anyone else. If He is our provider then we cannot lack. Behold, what manner of love is expressed by God through words that express His nature.

1. Elohim: "The Strong One"
2. Jehovah: "Lord"
3. El-Shaddai: "The All-Sufficient One"
4. Adonai: "Ownership"
5. Jehovah-Jireh: "The Lord Will Provide"
6. Jehovah-Nissi: "The Lord Our Banner"
7. Jehovah Shalom: "The Lord Is Peace"

John reminds us that God loves us so much that He would place us in His family. We don't have to enter the way the world does when adopting family members. We don't have to enter by being an offspring of parents, and we don't have to be concerned about entering through love that brings families together. Instead, we enter through the open door that God extends to us through His Son, Jesus Christ. Our salvation brings us directly into the family of God. We have been washed in the fountain, cleansed by His blood, and are joint-heirs with Jesus.

1 John 3:1: "Behold what manner of love the Father has bestowed on us, that we should be called children of God!"

There is a story told about a man who went to the hospital to see his son who was very ill. It was said that when the man arrived at his son's bedside, he read his Bible and prayed. Then he gently told his son that the doctors said his prognosis was dim and that he only had a few more days to live. So the father asked the boy whether he was afraid to meet Jesus. Blinking away a few tears, the little fellow said bravely, "No, not if He's like you, Dad." If only we knew the manner of His love!

Love Extraordinaire

Ephesians 2:3 declares that our nature was wrath during the time that we were sinners, and Romans 3:10-12 also declares that none of us is righteous, not one! We were made righteous through Jesus Christ. And John 15:13 reminds us that no one else has ever laid down his life for his friends.

Romans 5: 6-8: "You see, at just the right time, when we were still powerless, Christ died for the ungodly. Very rarely will anyone die for a righteous man, though for a good man someone might possibly dare to die. But God demonstrates his own love for us in this: While we were still sinners, Christ died for us" (NIV).

It wasn't that we were so loveable that He died for us. No, He died for the ungodly because of His manner of love that goes beyond all comprehension.

1 John 4:10: "In this is love, not that we loved God, but that He loved us and sent His Son to be the propitiation for our sins." There is nothing that we can do to add to what Christ did for us on the cross. The fact that He loves us as we are is beyond our natural reasoning.

No matter what our past record may have looked like, we were still given access to the kingdom of God through Christ. He took our place on the cross. That manner of love is still amazing, because He did not have to do it, but He did at all cost.

Unending and Everlasting

God's love is unending. We were loved, we are loved, and He will not stop loving us. Paul described this unending love in Romans 8:38-39: "For I am persuaded that neither death nor life, nor angels nor principalities nor powers, nor things present nor things to come, nor height nor depth, nor any other created thing, shall be able to separate us from the love of God which is in Christ Jesus our Lord."

Paul had no measuring rod to use that could go high enough nor deep enough nor wide enough nor far enough. God's love cannot be compared to anything He created, and He will not allow anything to separate us from His love.

Jeremiah 31:3: "The LORD appeared to us in the past, saying: 'I have loved you with an everlasting love; I have drawn you with lovingkindness'" (NIV).

God wants to remind us that even though the world may change, He does not change. He was and is and will forever be God (Heb. 13:8). He is the God who gives all or every good and perfect gift. The word that James uses for "change" is *parallage*, and the word for the "turn of the shadow," or as the NIV says it, "shifting shadows," is the word "tropic." Both words are used to show variations of nature such as length of days or the setting and place of the sun and moon in the sky.

James identifies the Lord as the Father of the heavenly lights.

Sometimes God is called light, as it is in 1 John 1:5. In this verse James is identifying God as the one who positions the sun, moon, and stars. Even though these things change often, God doesn't change. This is also what Hebrews 13:8 means when it says, "Jesus Christ is the same yesterday and today and forever."

God has given us so much to be thankful for, but most of all He has given us His Son and the chance to receive salvation. He didn't have to do that, but He delights in showing His manner of love as being the greatest love ever displayed and not to be compared by any other creature on this earth, not any other gods.

Chapter 4

Can God Fail Us?

Perhaps you are reading all these wonderful things about God's love and how great it is, but you are going through a fiery situation that has left you feeling down. You don't know where your next paycheck is coming from, and you don't know how you're going to send your kids to college or how you are going to clothe them. You don't know how you're going to put food on the table, and it seems as if you are being threatened from every side. You are too scared to answer the phone because you don't know what to say to your bill collectors.

Though you feel as if God has failed, you must realize that your human understanding has been blinded by the circumstances around you. It is important to watch these things and turn your eyes and mind to heavenly things and say what the Word says about your circumstances.

Peter's Encounter with Failure

In Matthew 14:22-36, Peter saw Jesus walking on the water and wondered if it was a spirit. He called out to Jesus, and Jesus told him not to be afraid. He called to Peter and told him to walk towards him, and Peter did.

When Peter saw the fierce winds he became afraid. He looked down, and he began to sink. He was afraid, and he called to the Lord to save him. Jesus stretched out His hand to Peter and helped him, but in verse 31 we read, "O thou of little faith, wherefore didst thou doubt?" Peter had the faith, until human reasoning took control. "Man is not capable of walking on water," Peter reasoned. As soon as his human reasoning superseded his faith, he began to sink!

The psalmist David declared his trust and confidence in God. He knew how to call upon the Lord in every situation. God was his shield, whether facing a giant or running for his life, he never turned his face from God.

Psalm 31:1-4

"In thee O Lord do I put my trust. Let me never be ashamed: deliver me in thy righteousness. Bow down thine ear to me, deliver me speedily, be thou my strong rock. Be a house of defense to save me.

For thou art my rock and my fortress; therefore for thy name's sake lead me and guide me. Pull me out of the net that they have laid privily for me; for thou art my strength" (verses 1-4, KJV).

"For my life is spent with grief and my years with sighing; my strength faileth because of mine iniquity, and my bones are consumed. I was a reproach among all mine enemies, but especially among my neighbors and a fear to mine acquaintance: they that did see me without fled from me. I am forgotten as a dead man out of mind: I am like a broken vessel. For I have heard the slander of many; fear was on every side: while they took counsel together against me, they devised to take away my life. But I trusted in thee O Lord: I said, Thou art my God" (verses 10-14, KJV).

Here the psalmist was a young man. Now let us look at a few verses in Psalms 71 and 73, where this same psalmist is older.

Psalm 71

"In thee, O Lord, do I put my trust: let me never be put to confusion. Deliver me in thine righteousness, and cause me to escape. Incline thine ear unto me, and save me. Be thou my strong habitation, whereunto I may continually resort; thou hast given commandment to save me for thou art my rock and my fortress. Deliver me, O my God, out of the hand of the wicked, out of the hand of the unrighteous and cruel man" (verses 1-4, KJV).

"Let my mouth be filled with thy praise and with thy honor all the day. Cast me not off in the time of old age; forsake me not when my strength faileth" (verses 8-9, KJV).

Psalm 73

"Truly God is good to Israel, even to such as are of a clean heart. But as for me, my feet were almost gone; my steps had well nigh slipped" (verses 1-2, KJV). In other words, a backslider is one of those people who know the Word of God but who slipped back into a world of sin.

"For I was envious at the foolish, when I saw the prosperity of the wicked" (verse 3, KJV).

The psalmist was saying that he didn't have the understanding and he was allowing human reasoning to take over. Comparing his life with the wicked, he became envious of them when he saw their prosperity.

Seemingly, we look at the things wicked people have and think they are doing so well. They may look well, but that does not mean they are doing well, but rather they are living in sin. They do not seem to have any problems in their home. They do not seem to have any financial problems, and you look at them and scream to the Lord, "My Lord, my feet are about to backslide. My hope, my strength, my faith is about gone!"

Now look at Psalm 73, starting with the fourth verse.

"For there are no bands in their death but their strength is firm. They are not in trouble as other men; neither are they plagued like other men. Therefore pride compasseth them as a chain; violence covereth them as a garment. Their eyes stand out with fatness; they have more than heart could wish. They are corrupt, and speak wickedly concerning oppression; they speak loftily. They set their mouth against the heavens, and their tongue walketh through the earth.. Therefore his people return hither; and waters of a full cup are wrung out to them" (verses 4-10, KJV).

Often believers, in our human reasoning, look at the people of the world thinking everything is going fine for them according to what we see in all their worldly possessions. The psalmist saw these people becoming wealthier and wealthier, and he said: "When I thought to know this, it was too painful for me until I went into the Sanctuary of God; then I understood their ends" (verse 16, KJV). In other words, it is only when he went into the sanctuary of God that he realized those people of the world were dying. It is in the sanctuary of the Lord that you can you experience spiritual understanding.

When you feel everything is becoming too much for you, you cannot control your children or your financial problems, and the weight of earthly cares become unbearable, there is one place for you to turn—the sanctuary of God. You need the Word of God to be a lamp unto your feet and a light unto your path. You know that you can always put your trust in God.

A Righteous God

The Bible says that the name of the Lord is a strong tower and the righteous run into it and are safe (Prov. 18:10). You need to know that you are God's chosen, God's righteous, God's peculiar people, even when you are going through the darkest valley and loneliest moments, when you feel no one cares, and you feel as if God cannot help you.

You must see God as He is, for He alone is God. He is Jehovah God; there is none like him. He's the alpha and the omega. He's the beginning and the end. He was here before the beginning. His beginning meets His end.

He's a continual, consuming God; flesh and blood cannot determine or declare who He is, how good He is, and how and when He goes into action. He is always good.

He is the same yesterday and today, and will be the same forever; He is a righteous and holy God. That's who He is. You must put your trust in Him. He is righteous. He is strong. You have more than a Samson when you have God.

When your enemies are coming like a flood, the Spirit will raise up a standard against them. You must know He's strong and that He is your rock in a weary land.

He Can Pull You Out

Through the history of this world people have tried to destroy the Word of God. The evolutionists and scientists have tried to destroy it. But Jesus said heaven and earth shall pass away but "My words will not fail." You can stand on the Word of God. It does not matter how bad things look today; you can stand on the Word of God.

Matthew 6:33 says, "Seek ye first the Kingdom of God and his righteousness, and all other things shall be added unto you!" (KJV). So when your mind tells you God cannot pull you out, I want you to say, "Devil, get behind me. Get thee behind me, Satan." Tell the Lord He is good and your trust is in Him.

You must say and believe He is a righteous God. You must say and believe He's your rock, your strong tower, your deliverer, your fortress, in Him will you trust! No matter what happens, He will pull you out!

God's promise of being with us constantly is contingent upon the principle that we obey Him and free ourselves from sinful deeds. In John 14:15 Jesus said," If ye love me, keep my commandments and I will pray the Father and He shall give you another comforter, that He may abide with you forever" (KJV).

Abiding forever is based upon you and me keeping His commandments. He also said that the world cannot receive the Comforter because He must indwell a believer—one who loves God and keeps His commandments. You cannot tie God to sin; sin must be dealt with before there is true fellowship with God.

In Joshua 1, God commissioned Joshua and established some parameters for success and His divine presence.

1. Everywhere you walk is yours.
2. No man will be able to stand before you all the days of your life.
3. God will not fail you.
4. Observe to do according to all the law.
5. Do not turn from the law; observe all that is written. Then you will have good success.

God told Joshua the things He would do for him and Israel first, then He gave them the conditions such as observe, keep, do, and do not turn. Joshua then commanded the armies of Israel to go forward, cross the Jordan, and experience God's awesome power. With this confidence, he then set his eyes on Jericho, obeying every word of the instructions he received from God. As Israel marched around the walls of Jericho, waiting on the command of their leader, every man was assured that God was with them and that they would win the battle.

The city of Jericho covered about eight acres. It was a fortress city, not just for its residents but also for the inhabitants of the nearby countryside. The walls may have been as much as thirty feet high and twenty feet thick. Jericho was considered to be invincible, being protected by the gods of the Canaanites, representing worldliness and sin. The capture of Jericho was the key to Joshua's whole war strategy, for it would demonstrate that Israel's God was superior to the gods of the Canaanites; hence the defeat of the Canaanites was necessary.

At the last sound of the trumpet and the shouts of the people, the walls fell flat. Surely God kept His Word!

Chapter 5

Can We Fail God?

We often talk about faith and about doubt being the opposite of faith. The prerequisite of faith is the absence of doubt. These two work against each other; sometimes we have faith and sometimes we have doubt, and we struggle with them. Most Christians only use faith when they are in trouble. "Lord, how am I going to pay my bills?"

It is the love of God that generates faith within us. Therefore, if we put our faith in God we will receive due reward, but if we doubt we will also receive the reward of our actions. Between faith and doubt, there is reasoning. The moment we begin to reason is the moment we begin to miss the mark.

Faith in Action

I recall once when I attempted to go to Colombia four times. Each time I tried, the Holy Spirit would restrain me. Then He said, "Go!" Before departing, I made contact with a pastor in Colombia. While speaking with him, he revealed to me that he had heard me speaking in Panama five years prior. The pastor said, "You spoke on 'The Power and the Potential of the Seed.' I will never forget that message, because it changed my life." The result was a church being planted in Colombia, and I was invited to preach there.

When I arrived, someone met me at the airport and took me to the hotel. I checked in and waited on the Lord. On the second day the pastor came, along with four other men. As we went along the way, things began to unfold. We met another pastor along the way, but he traveled in another taxi, so there were seven of us altogether. We proceeded through the crowded city of Bogotá where it was cold and rainy, until we came upon Hope Street and Thirteenth Avenue. At the corner of Hope Street, there was a bakery. The pastor said that was where we would have our meeting. It is important to put faith in action and go!

In our ministry, bread was always the symbol God gave me. Every church He used me to establish was confirmed with the sign of a bakery. We proceeded to park in front of the bakery, and as we got out of the car, I asked the pastor to take my picture in front of the bakery. When we finally walked into the bakery,

I felt tears begin to well up in my eyes. I tried to hide my emotions, because I did not want to draw attention to what God was doing just yet.

When something like that begins to happen in your life, you begin to realize that there is a shadow or presence around you. For me, that moment was the purpose for my plane landing and coming back, the purpose for me living in that moment. When God gave that present sign, I knew that I was in God's perfect will. I knew God had my back. He orchestrated everything so I would not have to worry.

God's confirmation was everywhere. The currency exchange rate for the U.S. dollar was twenty-six hundred pesos; the altitude of the city was twenty-six hundred feet above sea level, my room number was two, six, and six. Then I said, "Lord, what's with all the twenty-six?" He said, "Your words will influence half the population of the city." The city's population was twelve million people; that meant that I would be able to reach six million through the television ministry.

In addition, the Lord proceeded to tell me there was a widowed lady there with thirteen children. God wanted me to support them. Well, my wife and I were already supporting a woman with thirteen children in Colombia. This was yet another confirmation. The Lord said, "I have brought you here, and you will have influence over half the population. This is the reason I have kept you from coming, until now."

I do not know how you feel about your life, but I feel imprisoned; not that I am in physical bondage, but I am under the control of the Master that has the key for my life, for my coming in and going out.

Faith the size of mustard seed has the potential to move mountains. But nothing happens; not even one rock moves until you act on that faith. If you and I want to experience the many blessings of God through His promises, we must put our faith into action.

Let us look at the account of the twelve spies who were sent to spy out the land of Canaan (Num. 13:27-32). Take note that ten of the spies brought back an evil report. They were sent to a land that was flowing with milk and honey, but what they put the most emphasis on was the fact that "the people be strong that dwell in the land, and the cities are walled, and very great, moreover we saw the children of Anak [the giants] there" (verse 28).

Remember, these are people who had been told what to do and how to do it by God, and yet they were afraid to follow His instructions. The ten spies, who saw through natural eyes, had much to say, but it was all negative. They said things like, "We can't do it. We are not able. They are stronger than we." When you find yourself in the company of people who call themselves believers, but all that comes out of their mouths are unbelief and negativism, you need to find a different group to be your sphere of relationships.

Whose Report?

Caleb and Joshua, two of the twelve spies, gave a good report. Their report was full of faith and belief.

They knew what God had said, and they wanted to act on it. God told all of them, "I have given you the Promised Land" (Num. 13:2). Only two of them believed what God said. Those two looked at the circumstances surrounding them and still took God at His Word. Those two told the others in verse 30, "Let us go up at once and take the land because we're well able to do it."

The behavior of the ten spies shows us that people can know God's Word but still not really believe it. If they really believed what they read and are able to quote it at the drop of a hat, they should act on their belief.

Too many Christians want to sit around and say, "Lord, I believe. Please bless me," while doing absolutely nothing in the interim. Some people talk about what they believe in, yet they never do anything about it. James 2:17-18 says, "Even so faith, if it hath not works, is dead, being alone. Yea, a man may say, Thou hast faith, and I have works. Shew me thy faith without thy works, and I will shew thee my faith by my works" (KJV).

Caleb and Joshua were the only two adults of that entire generation to actually possess the Promised Land (Num. 14:29-38; Num. 26:65). These two young men could have easily allowed themselves to be persuaded to follow the actions of the others, some of them their elders. But they chose to follow God.

We cannot afford to rely only on our five senses—hearing, sight, smell, taste, and touch. In every situation all Christians should ask the question, "What does the Word of God say?" Then act on your faith in God's Word by obeying Proverbs 3:5, which instructs us to "Trust in the Lord with all thine heart; and lean not unto thine own understanding" (KJV). When you trust in the Lord with all your heart, there is no room left for doubt, unbelief, or disobedience. God does not take second best from anyone. If He can't have all of an individual, He doesn't want any part of that person. He requires to you serve Him with all of your mind, soul, and body.

When we start using our senses to try and reason out what God is telling us to do, we get ourselves in trouble. He wants us to trust Him with all our hearts and to not lean to our own understanding. If we refuse to act on God's Word, we can forget about receiving His blessings, because the Bible says that faith without works is dead!

In Luke 8:25, we find Jesus rebuking His disciples. He said to them, "Where is your faith?" He advised the disciples to get into a ship and go over to the other side of the lake, away from the multitude so they could get the rest their bodies needed. As the ship sailed away, Jesus went down in the bottom and fell asleep. A storm arose and beat against the ship, and the men became afraid. The disciples went down and awoke him, saying, "Master, master, we perish." What they were really saying to the Master was, "Here we are about to capsize and possibly die, and you are sound asleep." Christ arose and rebuked the wind and the raging water. The wind and the water became calm.

Everyone will be in a storm at some point in time. How we handle ourselves is a direct reflection of how firm our belief in God stands. Just because you are in a storm does not mean that God has failed you. It just might be that He has decided to allow Satan to fire his darts at you. If you lose faith and allow Satan to get your attention, it is you who have failed. Not God!

Gear Up!

Believers should wear the whole armor or of God daily, as instructed in Ephesians 6. Our loins should be wrapped up in truth, our breastplate must be of righteousness, and our feet covered and ready with the gospel of peace. Above all, we must have on the shield of faith that is not easily shaken by every wind that blows.

Our faith must be able to put out every fiery dart that the wicked one hurls our way. The helmet of salvation covers our head and preserves the knowledge that we learn as we earnestly study the Word of God. When we do this, we allow the sword of the Spirit to do its special work. Then, we must pray always "with all perseverance and supplication for all saints."

Take Your Rightful Position

Often we look at ourselves from the standpoint of what our physical eyes can see instead of what the Bible says belongs to us. When we do that, we cannot see the reality of what God has done for us because we are not seeing ourselves in Christ. We must see through His eyes and not ours. The ten spies saw with their natural eyes. When God sees that we are following the instructions left by His Son, He is overjoyed.

First Corinthians 1:30 says, "But of Him [God the Father] are ye in Christ Jesus, who of God is made unto us wisdom, and righteousness, and sanctification, and redemption" (KJV). God made Christ to bear sin for us; therefore, if you really want to be a successful believer, read the New Testament and see how many times you will find scriptures about our inheritance. Note those verses and confess them. Begin saying, "I am more than a conqueror in Christ Jesus. This is what I have in Christ!"

If these scriptures do not seem real to you now, keep confessing them. If you continue to confess God's Word about who you are and what you have in Christ, it will not be long before you will begin enjoying the reality of your benefits in Christ. Your first step is to know what God says that you can have through His Son, Jesus. Most people don't walk in the light of the Word because they don't know what the Word says.

Yes, You Can Succeed

It is quite evident that most believers do not really understand God's Word by the songs they sing that are not scriptural truths. For example, the song that says, "We're going to have rest, peace, and victory, when we get to heaven." The Word of God teaches us that we can have rest and peace now. We can have victory now! We don't have to wait until we get to heaven to enjoy these things; we can have them now.

God never fails, and He does not want His people to fail either. I believe His plan for us is to be victorious, and He gave us the ability to be overcomers in this life. Some believers think they do not have anything on this side of heaven except worry, misery, weakness, disappointment, and failure.

In Christ Jesus we do not have to fail! In Christ we do not have to feel the constant pangs of misery and our disappointments. Our worry can be turned into joy. Our weakness can be turned into strength—and our failure turned into success.

You can have peace in your heart, and you can have rest in your soul. But in order to get these things you must learn about Jesus. Not just know about Him but also have a personal relationship with Him. He said in Matthew 11:28-30, "Come unto me, all ye that labor and are heavy laden, and I will give you rest. Take my yoke upon you, and learn of me; for I am meek and lowly in heart: and ye shall find rest unto your souls. For my yoke is easy, and my burden is light" (KJV).

Complete in Him

I believe feeling incomplete is bombarding many believers in the body of Christ because they are failing to learn of Him! How do you learn of Him? Through His Word. The written Word has been given to us to learn about the living Word—Jesus Christ. Colossians 2:10 says, "And ye are complete in him, which is the head of all principality and power" (KJV). This is where many people miss their blessings when they say, "This verse is not referring to me. It cannot be, because I know I am complete."

Notice, the Bible did not say that you are complete in you. It says "ye are complete *in Him*." When you became a new creature through salvation, and the new birth, you are then complete. You may not be a grown-up Christian, but you are complete. If you died in this state, you would be in His presence.

There is a direct correlation between being complete as with physical and spiritual growth. When babies are born they are complete. They may have a deformity, but they are physically complete, though not grown. Well, the same is true about spiritual babies. They are not fully grown spiritually, but they are already complete because they are in Christ. If they live beyond that point, there is much growing that they will have to do, but that has nothing to do with the state of completeness they now have in Christ.

Being complete in Christ brings us to a place of rest in our spirit and lets us know that we can experience the greatness of God's love when we are assured that *He* cannot fail. His love is unending, we are protected by Him, and His promises are backed up by His Word that cannot return void.

Seek the Primary Source

Go to the primary source for your answers. Notice that David was not calling out to his soldiers or his family. He was calling out to God. That is not to say that God cannot use others in our lives to help us find answers, but ultimately, we need to turn to God as the source for our answers.

Jeremiah 33:3 says, "Call to Me and I will answer you and tell you great and unsearchable things you do not know."

Time spent in the Bible is time well spent, because as we gain familiarity with it, we see that God sometimes offers direct answers to our questions, and sometimes you will see general principles that you can apply to your situation or circumstance.

Sometimes God uses godly people to guide us or give us answers, because we do not always see things very clearly. Also, someone who has a continual relationship with God for a while has wisdom that others need. That wisdom comes from the Word of God. When asking God tough questions, we must be willing to receive His answers.

Always seek the right source. Do not go to an atheist, an agnostic, or a skeptic to learn about God. An atheist cannot tell me about a God he or she does not believe exists. An agnostic or skeptic can tell me nothing, except why they are questioning. Seek the primary source.

Jeremiah 29:13: "You will seek me and find me when you seek me with all your heart" (NIV). Hebrew 4:16: "Let us then approach the throne of grace with confidence, so that we may receive mercy and find grace to help us in our time of need" (NIV).

God is intensely interested not just in the world, but in you as an individual. And He invites you to come to Him whenever and wherever. Because He knows everything, and is everywhere all the time, you cannot get away from Him or His care for you. The apostle Paul says that God is only as far away as we can push Him. So go to Him and know that you cannot fail in Him because so great is His love for you!

Chapter 6

His Love Is Working in Us

As a pastor and counselor, I have learned that sometimes words are not sufficient when a person is experiencing human tragedy. At times I have felt so helpless in the presence of people who are at a moment beyond comfort. I have had to whisper a prayer for a word that would at least offer consolation and restore hope. However, time must take its course. We must remember that it is God who is working in us and that He will also bring us through. Philippians 2:13 says, "For it God which worketh in you both to will and to do his good pleasure" (KJV).

I recall having to counsel a dear sister who had just started attending our fellowship with her two young children when tragedy struck her life. She grew up as an only child, and despite what most people say about an only child being spoiled, it was not so in her household. After being educated in the best private schools and getting married, she found herself taking care of her parents. This was not easy for her own marriage, but one day matters became worse when her mother had a stroke, later had another one, and was paralyzed on both sides of her body.

This young lady never lost her faith in God through this entire period of sickness. She knew He is the greatest physician and that He would heal her mother, but it seemed like that was not to be any time soon. When her mother got worse, she took a medical leave of absence from her job, hoping she would be able to spend more time caring for her.

Then her father became ill with circulation problems. These wonderful grandparents had been the ones taking care of her children after school. One day her dad called to inform her that her mother was very ill, and later she died peacefully in her sleep. The daughter felt she had not done enough for her mother and started blaming God. She said He had failed her.

When I received this sad news, I was beside myself because it brought back memories of my own grief from the death of my grandmother and my father a few weeks apart. I, too, felt God had failed me. My grandmother had died peacefully in her sleep, and I felt as if I could not pray; I could not even go to church, I was so angry with God. My grandmother had no life insurance, and I had no savings to help. But thank God, even when I was angry with Him, He was still looking out for me.

God, I'm Angry with You!

It was not until after I met with my pastors that I realized that it was okay to be angry with God. I was embarrassed to have to tell my pastors that I felt this way about God, but I had to tell someone who could understand and guide me. After I repented I still had reservations; how could God take my grandmother from me?

After a time, I started working to rekindle my faith in God. I started to pray again, but it was still not the same. I would start praying and then I would start to cry and never finish the prayer. A week after my grandmother died, my father began having circulation problems. Having to go to the doctors and hospital again was just devastating for me. But I thank God that for His strength and the love of my children, I was able to go through that devastating trial.

The news from the doctor regarding my father was not good. He had no sensation in his lower leg, and I was told that his leg may have to be amputated in order to save his life since gangrene had set in. I prayed night and day; I prayed constantly. I cried out to God.

Another Disappointment with God!

I cried out to God again, "Why me? What have I done? What am I not doing?" I started reflecting back on my life to see if there were any stones that I had left unturned, to see if I had faltered along the way.

It just seemed as if God was giving me much more than I could bear. My big question was, "God, why are you putting me through this?"

My father's leg was amputated on my mother's birthday. What a remembrance—being there before my father went to surgery and there when he came out was the worst waiting period of my life. It reminded me of sitting in the consultation room at the hospital when the doctor came in and announced to my father and me that my grandmother had died.

After waiting for what seemed like ages, the doctor came and told me that everything went well and that he had amputated the leg. I was again angry with God. Why? Because I kept praying that when the doctor did the exploratory surgery, he would not have to amputate. How was I going to tell my father his leg was no longer there? Do you know what that does to one's pride? As he lay there on the hospital bed, and I lifted the sheet and saw there was no leg, I did not have the heart to tell him. I came home and cried my heart out.

I discovered two days later that the lady across the hall from my father's room in the hospital had had the same circulation problem. She died the day following her surgery from a blood clot to the lung. The news hit me like a two-edged sword. I saw the danger and how close to death's door my father had come, and I praised God for sparing his life and for taking him through the surgery and recovery.

He bounced back, and within two weeks he transferred to rehabilitation. It pained me to see him go through all the rigid exercises. He was the best in his group. He did what he was told and followed the therapist's instructions.

Dad hated the hospital, hated the food, hated the surroundings, and just plain wanted to come home. He had been through a lot, and his main goal was to drive again. This goal was soon to be fulfilled. His leg healed wonderfully, and I started praising God again.

My dad was home with me and hopping around, but it seemed that deep down he was grieving silently. His leg was totally healed, and he was getting ready to be fitted for his prosthesis. To me, he seemed to be looking forward to this because he told me I could start thinking about going back to work soon and he would be able to pick up the kids from school. They were his pride and joy, especially my son. They were very close.

In February 1999, I got a funny feeling that something was not right. It is amazing how the Holy Spirit works through us and in us. After taking the kids to school, I called home, but my father did not answer the phone. I tried several more times and got the same results. Finally, on the fourth attempt, he answered with a vibrant voice. In a split second, I could hear a rumbling as if the phone fell to the floor. I was about ten minutes away, so I rushed home, opened the door, and called out to him, but he was not in the chair where I had left him only a half-hour before.

I then heard him calling to me from the family room. I rushed there and found him looking pale. He said, "I can't tell you what happened. I don't know what happened to me, but I am going to die. I cannot breathe." Fear gripped me as I dialed 911. It seemed like forever before someone answered. When I got someone on the telephone, I tried to tell her what was happening. When I tried talking to my dad he kept telling me, "I am going to die, I can't breathe, I can't explain to you what happened."

Within four minutes, he stretched out his hand towards me, clenched his face, and just gave me a blank stare. I started shouting, "Dad, can you hear me? Daddy, daddy, daddy!" My father could no longer hear me...he was dead. This, I thought, could not be happening. My grandmother had just died four weeks earlier. How could God take my daddy too? I felt defeated and knew for sure that God was no longer good to me. I felt betrayed, and I felt disappointed in God. I thought that He had definitely failed me this time.

In His Timing

While dealing with my grief one day, the Holy Spirit placed these words in my spirit: "Thy purpose Lord we cannot see, all is well that is done by thee." The comfort these words brought to me was indescribable; they put so much peace in my heart. I was not seeing my dad in my dreams, and I prayed to God for some enlightenment that he was fine. Very soon after that, I saw my dad and grandmother in a vision, singing and praising God. Once again, the Holy Spirit assured me that they were happy. I saw that they were rejoicing, and this gave me inner peace.

Soon I started buying different books on faith, overcoming the loss of a loved one, and dealing with grief. However, I only found those books bringing me into a deeper and deeper depression. My greatest comfort came when I started to trust in God again. Slowly my faith began to return, even though I had some really down days, but God always pulled me through. "Call unto me, and I will answer thee, and show thee great and mighty things, which thou knoweth not" (Jer. 33:3 KJV).

Looking back over the past years, I remember that I always had praying, loving, compassionate parents. Prayers and devotion were standard in our home when I was growing up. Since the death of my father, I have been on a faith journey, and I am learning with each new day to put my faith and trust in God. By taking this faith journey I have opened myself up to God's guidance and direction. I realize now that God works everything out in His own time and not mine.

It has not been easy to get to this point in my life; it has been a struggle and is still a struggle. The strength that I have found is only available through God. My experience was unique and very scary. I know only time and God could be my healer. I have learned to hold on to God's promises while He is still working in me.

Chapter 7

How to Maintain Hope

Remember God knows the end from the beginning, and failure was not in His plan for you. His purposes are preordained. He knows the future and you must trust His long-term view. Here are a few keys that will help you in maintaining hope in the Lord.

1. "I am Alpha and Omega, the beginning and the end, saith the Lord, which is, which was, and which is to come, the Almighty" (Rev. 1:8 KJV).
2. God has set in place the specifics for your fulfillment of His purpose, and He knows what's best for you.
   "And we know that all things work together for good to them that love God, to them who are called according to his purpose" (Rom. 8:28).

"For the Lord God is a sun and shield: the Lord will give grace and glory: no good thing will he withhold from them that walk uprightly" (Ps. 84:11).

"If ye then, being evil, know how to give good gifts unto your children, how much more shall your Father which is in heaven give good things to them that ask him?" (Matt.7:11 KJV).

3. Your timing may not be God's timing. He works in His own time.

    "To every thing there is a season, and a time to every purpose under the heaven" (Eccles. 3:1).

    "And let us not be weary in well doing: for in due season we shall reap if we faint not" (Gal. 6:9 KJV).

4. Every distraction is a potential detour to what God wants.

    "Then the people of the land weakened the hands of the people of Judah, and troubled them in building. And hired counselors against them, to frustrate their purpose, all the days of Cyrus king of Persia, even until the reign of Darius king of Persia" (Ezra 4:4-5).

5. What you may consider a trial is God's way of strengthening you.

    "Wherein ye greatly rejoice, though now for a season, if need be, ye are in heaviness through manifold temptations: That the trial of your faith, being much more precious than of gold that perisheth, though it be tried with, fire, might be found unto praise and honor and glory at the appearing of Jesus Christ" (1 Pet. 1:6-7 KJV).

6. Jesus overcame in the hour of God's seeming abandonment, by a spirit of obedience. Develop in yourself that spirit of obedience.

   "And being found in fashion as a man, he humbled himself and became obedient unto death, even the death of the cross" (Phil 2:8).

   "And he went a little farther, and fell on his face and prayed, saying. O my Father, if it be possible, let this cup pass from me: nevertheless not as I will, but as thou wilt" (Matt. 26:39 KJV).

7. Stop looking at the water! Remember, Peter began to sink as he looked down at the waves.

   "And he said, Come. And when Peter was come down out of the ship, he walked on the water, to go to Jesus. But when he saw the wind boisterous, he was afraid; and beginning to sink, he cried, saying, Lord, save me" (Matt. 14:29-30 KJV).

8. Gird yourself up like a man! God wants you to reason with Him, confront God with your situation.

   "Gird up now thy loins like a man: for I will demand of thee, and answer thou me" (Job 38:3 KJV).

9. God knows what's best for you.

   "For it is God which worketh in you both to will and to do of His good pleasure" (Phil. 2:13 KJV).

10. Reason with God only. Present your situation to Him.

I love you, O LORD, my strength.
The LORD is my rock, my fortress and my deliverer; my God is my rock, in whom I take refuge. He is my shield and the horn of my salvation, my stronghold.
I call to the LORD, who is worthy of praise, and I am saved from my enemies.
The cords of death entangled me; the torrents of destruction overwhelmed me.
The cords of the grave coiled around me; the snares of death confronted me.
In my distress I called to the LORD; I cried to my God for help. From his temple he heard my voice; my cry came before him, into his ears.
(Ps. 18:1-6 NIV)

Remind God of His Promises

Jesus lived a life of fulfilling the Father's promises; no matter how many there were, He said yes to all of them. The very last one He fulfilled was His own death, burial, and resurrection. We also have a right to hold on to the promises in the Word of God, which never returns void.

His promises are not determined by human ability to understanding how He is going to fulfill them or when, but they are sure to be revealed if the mouth of the Lord hath spoken them! You must hold on to the promises of God and believe them. The following are some of the many promises of God designed for those who would believe what He says about who we are in Him.

Who Am I?

I am a child of God (Rom. 8:15-16).
I am redeemed from the hand of the enemy (Ps. 107:2).
I am forgiven (Col. 1:13-14).
I am saved by grace through faith (Eph. 2:18).
I am justified (Rom. 5:1).
I am sanctified (1 Cor. 6:11).
I am a new creature (2 Cor. 5:17).
I am a partaker of His divine nature (1 Pet. 1:4).
I am redeemed from the curse of the law (Gal. 3:13).
I am delivered from the power of darkness (Col. 1:13).
I am led by the Spirit of God (Rom. 8:14).
I am a son of God (Rom. 8:14).
I am kept in safety wherever I go (Ps. 91:11).
I am getting all my needs met by Jesus (Phil. 4:19).
I am casting all my cares on Jesus (2 Pet. 5:7).
I am strong in the Lord and in the power of His might (Eph. 6:10).
I am doing all things through Christ who strengthens me (Phil. 4:13).
I am an heir of God and joint heir with Christ Jesus (Rom. 8:17).
I am an heir to the blessings of Abraham (Rom. 8:17).

So Great Is His Love

I am observing and doing the Lord's commandments (Deut. 28:13).

I am blessed coming in and blessed going out (Deut. 28:6).

I am an heir of eternal life (1 John 5:11-12).

I am blessed with all spiritual blessings (Eph. 1:3).

I am healed by His stripes (1 Pet. 2:24).

I am exercising my authority over the enemy (Luke 10:19).

I am above and not beneath (Deut. 28:13).

I am more than a conqueror (Rom 8:37).

I am establishing God's Word here on earth (Matt. 16:19).

I am an overcome by the blood of the Lamb and the word of my testimony (Rev. 12:11).

I am daily overcoming the devil (1 John 4:4).

I am not moved by what I see (2 Cor. 4:18).

I am walking by faith and not by sight (2 Cor. 5:7).

I am casting down vain imaginations (2 Cor. 10:4-5).

I am bringing every thought into captivity (2 Cor. 10:4-5).

I am being transformed by the renewing of my mind (Rom. 12:1-2).

I am a laborer together with God (1 Cor. 3:9).

I am the righteousness of God in Christ (2 Cor. 5:21).

I am an imitator of Jesus (Eph. 5:1).

I am the light of the world (Matt. 5:14).

I am blessing the Lord at all times and continually praising Him with my mouth (Ps. 34:1).

How God Works

The first thing to remember is that God is involved in our sufferings. Although Satan is the god of this world, he is able to afflict our lives only by the permissive will of God (Job 1–2). He has promised in His Word that He will not allow us to be tried above what we are able to bear (1 Cor. 10:13).

God has also promised to bring good out of all the sufferings and persecution of those who love Him and obey His commandments (Rom. 8:28). Joseph recognized this truth in his own life and suffering (Gen. 50:20).

Hebrews 12:5 shows how God uses the painful experiences of our lives for our growth and benefit. God has also promised to stand by us in our pain, to walk with us through the valley of the shadow of death (Ps. 23:4; Isa. 43:2). He does so by His Holy Spirit, who comforts us in all our trouble. He sends sufficient grace to each one of His children so that they can bear the trials of life (1 Cor. 10:13).

Remember that the Lord Jesus shares your pain; as we pray to Him we have a sympathetic High Priest who himself experienced the various dimensions of our trials and sufferings (Heb. 4:15). He has indeed borne our griefs and carried our sorrows (Isa. 53:4); there is healing for our own sufferings through the sufferings that he bore on our behalf (Isa. 53:5 KJV).

Victory over Personal Suffering

Believe that God cares deeply for you regardless of how severe your circumstances (Rom. 8:36; 2 Cor. 1:8-10; James 5:11; 1 Pet. 5:7). Suffering should never lead you to deny God's love for you or to reject Him as your Lord and Savior.

Turn to God in earnest prayer and seek His face, wait upon Him until He delivers you from your affliction (Ps. 21:8-14; 40:1-3).

Expect God to give you the grace that is necessary to bear your affliction until deliverance comes (1 Cor. 10:13). Always remember that we are conquerors through him who loved us (Rom. 8:37; John 16:33). The believer's faith lies not in the removal of weakness and suffering but in the manifestation of divine power through human weakness (2 Cor. 4:7).

Read the Word of God, especially Psalms 11, 16, 23, 27, 40, 46, 61, 91, 121, 125, and 138; they give comfort in times of affliction.

Seek revelation and discernment from God regarding your particular situation through prayer, the scriptures, the enlightenment of the Holy Spirit, or the counsel of a godly and mature believer.

If your suffering is physical in nature, follow the steps as outlined in the Word: Psalm 103:1-5; Luke 4:18, Luke 5:17-26; and James 5:14-15. Throughout Jesus' life on earth, His threefold ministry was teaching God's Word, preaching repentance from sin, and healing every kind of sickness, disease, and infirmity among the people (Matt. 4:23-24).

During the time of our suffering, remember the prediction of Christ that you will suffer trouble and affliction in your life as a believer (John 16:33).

Look forward, with eager anticipation, to that time when God shall wipe away all tears from their eyes; and there shall be no more death, neither sorrow, nor crying, neither shall there be any more pain (Rev. 21:4)

Conclusion

If you have never trusted in Christ as your Savior, will you do that right now?

First, you need to recognize that you are a sinner deserving punishment. It's a fact of life, because the Bible says we are all sinners, whether we know it or not, whether we fully understand it or not. So acknowledge that you need a Savior.

Second, believe that Jesus died on the cross for you, shedding His blood for your forgiveness, and rose again from the dead.

And thirdly, call on Him to save you for heaven. The Bible says that all who call on the name of the Lord will be saved. Admit your need, believe Jesus died and rose, and then call on Him.

If you can make this confession today, then you are on the right road that will lead you each day into a greater awareness of the greatness of God's love for you. It will be the best understanding of God that you will ever need.

www.ingramcontent.com/pod-product-compliance
Ingram Content Group UK Ltd.
Pitfield, Milton Keynes, MK11 3LW, UK
UKHW041944230426
12048UKWH00008B/116